Can a Christian not be homophobic?

onmounty and Aleh Nahorny

Published by Aleh Nahorny, 2024.

CAN A CHRISTIAN NOT BE HOMOPHOBIC?

First edition. October 9, 2024.

ISBN: 979-8227182678

Written by onmounty and Aleh Nahorny.

Table of Contents

Table of Contents

Who is this book for?

Who is this book for?

Strictly speaking, I wrote a book that I wish I had read myself years ago. I remember arguing with a peer in high school about homosexuality. What I didn't know at the time was that it wasn't a theoretical question for him. I had not researched this topic before. But I discovered that I already had a ready-made, somehow magically formed, opinion about it. The short form was that homosexuality is a disorder, a deviation from the norm. And I could prove it (it seemed to me) on all levels: biological, social, theological.

It seemed obvious to me that, on a biological level, sex is for reproduction. However, homosexual couples cannot have children. This means that it is not biologically normal. I didn't know then that even in the animal world, sex is not only used to produce offspring. And then I didn't know that evolution was concerned with the survival of a population, not the genes of a particular individual. However, work demonstrating the benefits of homosexual individuals in increasing the adaptive capacity of a population has only recently appeared.

It seemed obvious to me that gay couples threaten to destroy the institution of the family. And children growing up in homosexual families will be morally and psychologically damaged. I made these assumptions "out of thin air" As I now know, all relevant scientific research proves otherwise.

But most firmly was my theological conviction that homosexuality is an abomination in the eyes of God. After all, the Bible speaks about this very clearly and unambiguously!

Oh, if only I had been given this book to read! Perhaps then my ignorant self-confidence would not have added fuel to the fire of the inner conflict of the interlocutor, who was looking for harmony between his natural sexuality and his love for God!

I hope that this book will be useful, especially to those godly people who recognize themselves in the descriptions of the views of my youth.

Second, it is for people of faith and non-believers who stand up for the equal rights of queer people. Here they will find a reasoned shield against theological attacks on queer people. I am convinced that equal rights for queer people in Christian churches is not just a demand of the "outside broken world", as the homonegativists say. A healthy approach to biblical theology also requires this.

Ultimately, it is for queer people trying to resolve the conflict between their sense of identity and their Christian faith.

What exactly is this book about?

The debate about LGBT+ raises many questions and has many branches. But the only question that can be relevant to the theological conclusion is, "Do LGBT+ beliefs and practices hinder salvation?"
Therefore, I support opponents of queer theology who the soteriological quotation of the New Testament consider central in this discussion:

> "You know that wicked people will not inherit the kingdom of God, don't you? Stop deceiving yourselves! Sexually immoral people, idolaters, adulterers, male prostitutes, homosexuals, thieves, greedy people, drunks, slanderers, and robbers will not inherit the kingdom of God." (1 Corinthians 6:9-10)

Later we will see if it is correct to translate 'arsenokoites' from the Apostle Paul's letters as homosexual. For now, let's note that it is from the perspective of salvation that I will try to engage in the discussion.

> "Now that we have been justified by his blood, how much more will we be saved from wrath through him!" (Romans 5:9)

Everything else in Christianity, from ethical standards to liturgical traditions, is a means of joining Christ's gift of salvation. Or, in the interpretation of some denominations, they are signs of inclusion in salvation. So it is no exaggeration to say that the core of Christian theology is soteriology — the doctrine of salvation.

Whether we personally like or dislike the way of life of our loved ones, the style of clothing, the choice of profession, the choice of a spouse... even the image of piety is none of our business!

> "Who are you to criticize someone else's servant? His own Lord will determine whether he stands or falls. And stand he will, because God is able to make him stand". (Romans 14:4)

The only time we have the right to rebuke is when we learn that what others publicly preach as the Christian norm is actually an obstacle to salvation. In this case, we are encouraged to share our concerns and arguments so that others can consciously and freely decide what they think is right and what path they want to take.
But:

> "Everything you do should be done in love!" (1 Corinthians 16:14)

Before we go any further, we should make sure we understand each other. Therefore, I will first explain in what sense I will use the main words and terms.

Homosexuality

The LGBT+ phenomenon is too diverse. I don't plan to cover it all in this short study. Although I will offer general methodological principles with the help of which you can further analyze any phenomenon of the LGBT+ spectrum. In this book, I will focus on homosexuality because it is the most popular and discussed phenomenon.
Keep in mind that when I write about homosexual relationships, I do not mean any same-sex relationships, but only relationships of committed lifelong love between equal partners.
Why am I not interested in other homosexual relationships? Because a relationship based on sinful motives or obviously accompanied by sins (infidelity, humiliation of a partner, etc.) leads to eternal destruction,

even if it is a heterosexual relationship. That is, an analysis of such a homosexual partnership does nothing to clarify whether the homosexual nature of this relationship, rather than the accompanying sins, hinders salvation.

Queer Theology

You can find many external and internal definitions of queer theology in literature. I ask the reader to stay away from them while reading this book. Here, queer theology is a term that summarizes various schools of theological thought that suggest that homosexual relationships, as they are not accompanied by other sins, are not an obstacle to salvation.

Queer theology is based on the belief that there is nothing in Scripture that condemns homosexual love relationships. And the texts that Christian fundamentalists use to defend the homonegative position are mistranslated and misunderstood.

Christianity

You know that Christianity is divided into many movements and denominations that cannot find a common language on many issues. The largest branches of Christianity are Orthodoxy, Catholicism and Protestantism. Already at this stage of classification, the problem of understanding soteriology arises.

To simplify, we can say that Catholicism preaches salvation by works and Protestantism by faith. Both of these approaches are united only by the fact that they are based on a legal understanding of the problem of salvation. The sacrifice of Christ is necessary because God somehow cannot ignore the demands of justice, and so that sinners do not have to pay for their sins in eternity, the absolute Righteous God-man Jesus Christ pays for the guilty. That is, Christ's Sacrifice is a substitutionary sacrifice — the satisfaction of God's justice.

> "For as by one man's disobedience many were made sinners, so by one man's obedience many will be made righteous" (Rom. 5:19) By his obedience unto death, Jesus accomplished the

> substitution of the suffering Servant, who "makes himself an offering for sin", when "he bore the sin of many", and who "shall make many to be accounted righteous", for "he shall bear their iniquities" (Is. 53:10-12) Jesus atoned for our faults and made satisfaction for our sins to the Father." (Catechism of the Catholic Church, 615.)
>
> "We unanimously believe, teach, and confess that Christ is our Righteousness neither according to the divine nature alone nor according to the human nature alone, but that it is the entire Christ according to both natures, in His obedience alone, which as God and man He rendered to the Father even unto death, and thereby merited for us the forgiveness of sins and eternal life, as it is written: As by one man's disobedience many were made sinners, so by the obedience of One shall many be made righteous, Rom. 5:19.
>
> Accordingly, we believe, teach, and confess that our righteousness before God is (this very thing], that God forgives us our sins out of pure grace, without any work, merit, or worthiness of ours preceding, present, or following, that He presents and imputes to us the righteousness of Christ's obedience, on account of which righteousness we are received into grace by God, and regarded as righteous." (Book of Concord. III. The Righteousness of Faith Before God.)

But I belong to the Eastern Orthodox Christian tradition. Here the problem of salvation is revealed in a more multifaceted and complex way. In the next chapter, I will try to explain as simply and briefly as possible from which understanding of salvation all further analysis of LGBT issues originates. I request Christians of other faiths and denominations to read this chapter carefully. I will try to appeal only to the texts of the Holy Scriptures and avoid discussing controversial issues to the extent that they are not relevant to the purposes of this book. But I ask each reader to decide for himself how far his Christian conscience and the theology of his Church can agree with the arguments of this chapter.

In any case, when I write about Christianity, Christian attitudes, and the like, keep in mind that while I try to make generalizations that are difficult for any Christian to argue with, I am primarily referring to Orthodox Christianity. Be careful: the doctrine of your particular Church may differ from my generalizations!

More universal are the chapters that analyze the biblical texts on which fundamentalists base the sinfulness of homosexuality.

Here I present objective arguments that, regardless of the reader's confessional affiliation, lead to the conclusion that there is no text in the Holy Scriptures that clearly and unequivocally condemns homosexual faithful love between equal partners, unless such relationships are associated with other sins.

However, I must warn you that the conclusions I have drawn are not the official teaching of my Church. Strictly speaking, in Orthodoxy, the theological analysis of this problem has not been carried out by any church body whose opinion is generally binding on the whole Church. However, due to various external reasons, a homonegativist reading of the Bible and the Holy Fathers dominates. Therefore, it can be said that in this book I dispute the beliefs of the majority of my coreligionists.

Unacceptable arguments

I will say a few words about arguments that are often used by homonegativists, but which are not worth paying attention to.

I will not talk about the historical tradition of the Church's approach to homosexuality. First, because this tradition is not reflected in dogmatic teaching, and therefore belongs to those questions that are not immutable and can be debated.

Secondly, the homonegativists themselves are often not well aware of this tradition or deliberately falsify it. For example, my coreligionists often refer to canonical rules or quotes from saints, where it is mentioned in Russian 'мужеложство' [muzhelozhstvo]. According to them, homosexual behavior is meant in all these cases. However, reading the Greek source shows that this one Russian word means a variety of things, from pederasty (in the old sense of relations with boys) to anal intercourse (not necessarily homosexual).

Third, ethical progress is a normal and, so to speak, traditional process in the Church's view. Christians form their ethical views by correlating their knowledge of the world with their understanding of the spirit of the Bible's teaching.

> “Every word or deed must be supported by the testimony of inspired Scripture... and what is known from nature and from the customs of public life must be used to confirm what we do or say.” (Saint Basil the Great. Moral Rules, Rule 26.)

Both the first and the second changed throughout history. Ideas about the structure of the world cannot be static, at least because of the development of scientific knowledge. The understanding of the spirit of the Gospel deepens as Christian communities develop morally and, accordingly, are prepared to understand God's word on a new level.

> "I still have a lot to say to you, but you cannot bear it now. Yet when the Spirit of Truth comes, he will guide you into all truth. For he will not speak on his own accord, but will speak whatever he hears and will declare to you the things that are to come." (John 16:12-13)

This, of course, is also facilitated by the development of biblical and theological sciences.

For this reason, the development of Christian ethics cannot remain stagnant either. This means that the argument: "This is how the Church has viewed this issue in the past" is not enough in ethical matters. It is necessary that during this time there is no progress in science and theology that could affect the approach to the problem at hand.

Here's an example. In ancient times, the unproductive discharge of a man's sperm was almost tantamount to murder. People did not know then that to form the human body, information from the mother and father must be combined. They believed that only the male seed had a formative, creative power. They perceived the mother's body only as the soil from which the grains draw materials and nutrients for growth and development.

> "The male and the female differ from each other in the possession of an ability and in the lack of an ability. The male is able to concoct, formulate and to ejaculate the sperm which contains the origin of the form [of the being to be born]-I do not mean here the material element out of which it is born resembling its parent but the initiating formative principle whether it acts within itself or within another. The female, on the other hand, is that which receives the seed but is unable to

> formulate or to ejaculate it." (Aristotle. On the Generation of Animals.)

Therefore, forms of sexual intimacy in which the male seed does not enter the soil of the mother's womb were condemned in much the same way that Christians today condemn abortion. Ancient Jews and Christians believed that only an obsession with excessive sexuality could lead to the deliberate killing of a potential baby to obtain another dose of sexual pleasure. (This knowledge will come in handy when we discuss the letter to the Romans.)

However, modern science (genetics and embryology) knows that human life as a biological individual begins with the fusion of the nuclei of male and female germ cells and the formation of a single nucleus containing unique genetic material. Therefore, modern Christians defend the child's right to life, not from the moment the man throws his seed, but from the moment of conception.

Ancient Churches have the hardest time changing their views. After all, their library has accumulated many quotes from authors authoritative to them that reflect outdated views. There will always be parishioners who will not understand why the ancient saint so morally evaluated this or that phenomenon. They will simply accuse modern theologians of modernism and apostasy. This is why the ancient churches were so slow and reluctant to revise their moral codes. However, even in very conservative Eastern Orthodoxy, we are already seeing concessions to non-abortive methods of contraception.

> "The Orthodox Church has no dogmatic objection to the use of safe and non-abortifacient contraceptives within the context of married life, not as an ideal or as a permanent arrangement, but as a provisional concession to necessity." ("For The Life Of The World. Toward a Social Ethos of the Orthodox Church" — a document prepared by the Theological Commission of the Ecumenical Patriarchate.)

I do not think that the authors of the document have any dogmatic reasons not to consider non-abortive methods of contraception as permissible in married life without any reservations. I think they don't list these reasons in the document because of their absence. But the sudden leap from condemning unproductive male ejaculation as murder to fully embracing non-abortively contraceptives would be too shocking for many believers. Therefore, I think, diplomatic wording is used to soften the blow, that contraceptives are accepted, but with reservations that are not specified.

From this example, we understand that even in the most conservative Churches, the code of ethics is revised, developed, and changed. And that's normal!

Nor will I refute the claim of homonegativists that homosexuality is not an innate but an acquired trait.

First, it's as pointless as arguing with flat-earthers. In order for the interlocutor to understand you, you need a culture of scientific thinking. However, the very fact that the interviewer advocates anti-science nonsense shows that, at least on this issue, he refuses to utilize the culture of scientific thinking.

Second, this book deals with the theological rather than the scientific side of the question. And for theological analysis and moral evaluation, it does not matter whether innate or acquired qualities lead people to develop love relationships with members of their own sex. Man was created in the image of God. This means that he has the God-given ability to creatively transform the world. In the human world, 'unnatural' does not automatically mean bad, sinful. Look around — man lives almost entirely in a world of man-made objects and culture. It is not a natural instinct that drives homonegative Christians to marry or build temples. Animals satisfy their sexual instincts without the institution of marriage. And even supposing that man had an innate religious instinct, the pagans satisfied it among natural objects. Against nature to build special buildings to satisfy him.

When I hear that homosexual people are distorting who God created them to be, I am reminded that God created us to be capable and called us to perfect our natural qualities. Doesn't the Bible say that we are born with an innate tendency to sin, called the 'old man'? Doesn't the Bible call us to overcome the 'old man' to become the 'new man' in Christ? So to say that any opposition to one's nature for any idea is bad is not possible! Isn't the idea of the sanctity of marital fidelity causing homonegative Christians to suppress their innate natural instincts toward other women?

Therefore, even someone who is convinced of the unnatural origin of homosexuality, before calling homosexuality sinful and unacceptable, must show how this sexual orientation hinders salvation in Christ.

The key to Heaven's gate is love

The main word in orthodox soteriology is 'deification' (Greek: θεοποίησις — becoming a god). Man was created in the image and likeness of God (Genesis 1:26), and his task is to become like God. "Be ye therefore perfect, even as your Father which is in heaven is perfect" (Matthew 5:48), Christ exhorts. Directing their will to God and accepting the grace of sanctification brought by Christ, people are adopted by God and become gods by grace.

> "But when the fullness of time had come, God sent his Son, born of a woman, born under the law, in order to redeem those who were under the law, so that we might receive adoption as his children. Now because you are his children, God has sent the Spirit of his Son into our hearts to cry out, "Abba! Father!" So you are no longer a slave but a child, and if you are a child, then you are also an heir through God." (Galatians 4:4-7)

Early Christian authors, who are venerated as saints in Orthodoxy, understood the work of salvation in the same way:

> "I said, You are all the sons of the Highest, and gods; but you shall die like men". He speaks undoubtedly these words to those who have not received the gift of adoption, but who despise the incarnation of the pure generation of the Word of God, defraud human nature of promotion into God, and prove themselves ungrateful to the Word of God, who became flesh for them. For it was for this end that the Word of God

was made man, and He who was the Son of God became the Son of man, that man, having been taken into the Word, and receiving the adoption, might become the son of God. For by no other means could we have attained to incorruptibility and immortality, unless we had been united to incorruptibility and immortality. But how could we be joined to incorruptibility and immortality, unless, first, incorruptibility and immortality had become that which we also are, so that the corruptible might be swallowed up by incorruptibility, and the mortal by immortality, that we might receive the adoption of sons?" (Irenaeus of Lyons. Against Heresies. Book III, Chapter 19.)

"For He has become Man, that He might deify us in Himself, and He has been born of a woman, and begotten of a Virgin, in order to transfer to Himself our erring generation, and that we may become henceforth a holy race, and partakers of the Divine Nature, as blessed Peter wrote (2 Peter 1:4)." (Athanasius the Great. Letter LX. To Adelphius, Bishop and Confessor: against the Arians.)

One of the tenets of Christian theology is that "God is love, and whoever abides in love abides in God, and God in him" (1 John 4:16). Therefore, the practical path to deification, likeness to God, acceptance to God lies precisely in love. The ability to love and receive love is the real key to salvation!

Love, in a sense, reconciles the long-standing debate about salvation by faith or works. Not just any faith saves, but "faith working through love" (Galatians 5:6).

On the other hand, any pious acts, ascetic acts, and even acts of mercy without love are soteriological nothingness.

> "If I speak in the tongues of humans and angels but have no love, I have become a reverberating gong or a clashing cymbal. If I have the gift of prophecy and can understand all secrets and every form of knowledge, and if I have absolute faith so as to move mountains but have no love, I am nothing. Even if I give away all that I have and surrender my body so that I may boast but have no love, I get nothing out of it. Love is always patient, Love is always kind... There is no limit to her hope, And never will she fall. Love never fails. Now if there are prophecies, they will be done away with. If there are tongues, they will cease. If there is knowledge, it will be done away with." (1 Corinthians 13:1-8)

The whole point of the Old Testament commandments is about love for God and people: Matthew 22:35-39. Whatever virtues you invoke to save yourself, love is the essence and totality of all moral excellence.

> "Above all, clothe yourselves with love, which ties everything together in unity." (Colossians 3:14)

The Greek text here says that love is a στελειός (connection, union) τελειότητος. The latter word means perfection, completeness, completeness. Thus all virtues lead to love and find their consummation in it.

> "Because what gain is there, my children, if someone has everything, but does not have love which saves? For just as if someone were to make a great dinner in order to invite the King and the rulers, and were to prepare everything sumptuously, so that nothing might be lacking, but had no salt, would anyone be able to eat that dinner? Certainly not. But he would have lost everything he had spent and wasted all his hard work, and brought ridicule on himself from those

> he had invited. So it is in the present instance. For what advantage is there in toiling against winds, without love? For without it every deed, every action is unclean. Even if someone has attained complete chastity, or fasts, or keeps vigil; whether they pray or give banquets for the poor; even if they think of offering gifts, or first fruits, or offering; whether they build churches, or do anything else, without love all those things will be reckoned as nothing by God. For the Lord is not pleased by them." (St. Ephraim the Syrian. On Love)

The school of Christian love and the environment in which it unfolds are human relationships.

> "The person who says that he is in the light but hates his brother is still in the darkness. The person who loves his brother abides in the light, and there is no reason for him to stumble. But the person who hates his brother is in the darkness and lives in the darkness. He does not know where he is going, because the darkness has blinded his eyes. <...> Dear friends, if this is the way God loved us, we must also love one another. No one has ever seen God. If we love one another, God lives in us, and his love is perfected in us <...> Whoever says, "I love God," but hates his brother is a liar. The one who does not love the brother whom he has seen cannot love a God whom he has not seen. And this is the commandment that we have from him: the person who loves God must also love his brother." (1 John 2:9-11; 4:11-12, 20-21)

> "Love for God consists in love for neighbor, and he who cultivates in himself love for neighbor, together with it collects in his heart an unappreciated spiritual treasure — love

> for God." (St. Ignatius (Bryanchaninov). About salvation and perfection. — Translated from Russian)

I dare to think that believers of most Christian denominations would agree that the presence of divine love in a person's life (the apostle Paul describes its qualities in 1 Corinthians 13:4-8) is a sign that "he abides in God, and God in him" (John 4:16). Therefore, such a person is not deprived of the opportunity to receive a blessed eternal life, salvation.

When talking about deification through the experience of love, the Holy Fathers often recalled an ancient principle that also appears in Scripture (e.g., Romans 6:5; 1 John 3:2): "Like unites with like and repels the opposite" or "like is known by like". In the Bible, the word "know" often refers to the physical union of people (e.g., Genesis 4:1-2) and experiencing something personally (e.g., Isaiah 53:3, 59:8; Wisdom 3:13; Judges 3:1). It is precisely because God is love that anyone who loves as God does is united with Him and has the opportunity to be saved.

One path to saving likeness to God is the lifelong relationship we call conjugal love.

> "Through marriage we become one another's hands, ears, and feet. Marriage doubles what had been weak. It is a great joy to our friends, a distress to our enemies. Sorrows shared hurt less; joys shared are sweeter for both; wealth brings greater joy to those who are like-minded. To those who are in need, being like-minded brings greater joy than wealth. Marriage supplies a lock of self-control over desires and sets a seal on our natural need for friendship... It is a drink from the household spring from which strangers cannot taste; it does not flow forth outside nor can another collect it from outside. The mutual love of those who are united in the flesh and are of one soul sharpens their piety to a fine point." (St. Gregory of Nazianzus. Carmina [latin for 'Songs'].)

> "To save your soul is to learn to love. All that I said above - the Kingdom of God and receiving the grace of the Holy Spirit - is the same thing. After all, what is union with God, deification? We know the words of Apostle John the Theologian: God is love, and he who abides in love abides in God (1 John 4:7). That is, deification is a state when love becomes dominant in man. To the extent that man learns to love, to that extent he is fit for eternity <...> And again, in His prayer the Lord speaks to the Father about His disciples and repeats these words: May they all be one, as You Father in Me and I in You (John 17:21). This is what salvation is all about - in unity, not in outward unity, but in such a way that another's joy becomes your joy, another's pain becomes your pain <...> And family is the first step to such unity. Where really husband and wife are one flesh. After all, the ideal of love is when two people become one. And just the family is the organism in which two individuals, who were initially strangers to each other, should become one with one heart, one thought, in the image of the Holy Trinity, without losing their personal uniqueness, but enriching and complementing each other." (Igor Gagarin, priest. Reflections on marriage and family. — Translated from Russian.)

But is such a deep and committed same-sex love relationship possible? Please note that we are not yet asking whether same-sex couples can marry or have sex. At this stage, we ask, can there be a spiritual and psychological closeness between them that we would consider worthy of marriage if the lovers were of different sexes?

The Holy Scriptures provide the answer in the example of the love of the prophet and king David and Jonathan. After Jonathan's death, David made a very powerful statement over his body:

> "I am distressed for thee, my brother Jonathan: very pleasant hast thou been unto me: thy love to me was wonderful, passing the love of women." (2 Samuel 1:26)

David knew what he was talking about. He had several wives, so he had something to compare it to. However, his relationship with Jonathan was more intimate (spiritually and psychologically) and more precious to him than with any of the women. So, regardless of whether David had sexual relations with Jonathan or not, they had a close and deep relationship, no different from the heterosexual relationship considered worthy of a Christian marriage. Neither the authors of the Bible nor the holy commentators of the Holy Scriptures condemn this same-sex love between David and Jonathan.

Traditionalists emphasize that this is only male friendship. Very close, but friendship, not marriage! But what is conjugal love if not a close intimate friendship, just with the addition of sexual attraction?

This is where homonegativists and queer theologians draw the line between incompatible interpretations of the Bible. Both sides agree that same-sex friendships can be pleasing to God. However, homonegativists are convinced that the Bible condemns same-sex sexual attraction. Queer theologians claim that it is not in the Scriptures.

Before we take a closer look at the texts offered by homonegativists, let's pay attention to this fact: if it suddenly turns out that the Bible does not condemn same-sex sexual attraction, then the same-sex relationship of conjugal love is, soteriologically speaking, no worse than heterosexual love.

Why the Bible Doesn't Talk About Homosexuality

The main mistake made by those who try to find condemnation of homosexuality in the Bible is that they read the biblical texts without considering the cultural and historical context. Before we begin to analyze the standard passages, it makes sense to say that there are at least two good reasons why it is not useful to search the Bible for references to homosexuality.

First, in the history of societies associated with biblical culture until the 19th century, there was no phenomenon of homosexual love relationships between equal partners. In the culture of the nations that surrounded the prophets and apostles, homosexual acts were carried out either in the context of idolatrous cults, or in the context of prostitution, or in the context of temporary love affairs between older partners with younger ones, or between masters and slaves. Such relationships are unhealthy and sinful, regardless of whether they are heterosexual or homosexual.

Secondly, until the era of German Romanticism (that is, until the end of the 18th century), a woman and a man were not considered as persons of different sexes. In the ancient world, the philosophical model of nature prevailed, which can be called the mono-sexual model of Aristotle and Galen. Aristotle was one of the first to clearly formulate it, and Galen put a lot of effort into developing it. In their opinion, a woman is simply an underdeveloped man.

> "Now a boy is like a woman in form, and the woman is as it were an impotent male..." (Aristotle. On the Generation of Animals.)

> "As regards the individual nature, woman is defective and misbegotten, for the active force in the male seed tends to the production of a perfect likeness in the masculine sex; while the production of woman comes from defect in the active force or from some material indisposition, or even from some external influence; such as that of a south wind, which is moist, as the Philosopher [meaning Aristotle — ed.] observes (De Gener. Animal. iv, 2)." (Thomas Aquinas, Sum of Theology.)

Based on this view of men and women, it was believed that the proper role for men both in social life and in bed is to give, to be active, to lead, while women should be receptive, submissive, passive by nature.

> "Man is by nature the object of action, and woman is the subject of action. Authority and obedience are not only necessary but beneficial, and from birth some creatures are inclined to obedience, others to authority. So is the relationship between man and woman: the first is naturally superior, the second inferior, so the first is dominant and the second is subordinate." (Aristotle. Politics.)

> "The soul plays the role of the artist, and the body is the instrument, because the body is the object of action... as matter, for example, the object of action is the woman because the action is directed at her, and the action is adultery, fornication, or lawful cohabitation." (Nemesius, bishop of Emesa. On Human Nature. Orig.: Περὶ φύσεως ἀνθρώπου)

Delving into the cultural and historical context is important for a proper understanding of the biblical texts. We must remember that the authors of the Bible did not divide sexual acts into homosexual and heterosexual. To them, they were all homosexuals. They were only concerned that men should not demean their full masculinity by their passive and submissive behavior. On the other hand, it was considered unnatural and sinful for the defective female nature to be active and dominant over the male.

However, we find no direct mention in the Bible of lifelong loving relationships between partners of equal social and natural status that were accompanied by sexual intimacy. Perhaps there were isolated rare examples of such coexistence. However, until the 20th century, they did not exist as a social phenomenon and were not perceived as an ethical problem worthy of attention.

It was also not known that sexual orientation is an innate phenomenon. The first speculations about it appeared in the 19th century at the end of the 20th century at the beginning. In the culture of that time, it was believed that men and women were a priory bisexual (translated into the language of our time). For example, in the apostolic age a man could have a wife and children but still have fun with a young man-lover or man-slave.

Therefore, if the biblical text mentions sexual acts between persons of the same sex, we must remember that the authors do not associate them with homosexuality in the sense of sexual orientation. Therefore, innate sexual attraction to members of one's own sex does not affect the moral and ethical evaluation of such actions. We must look to other guidelines that were significant to the authors of the books of the Bible.

"Male and female created He them" — Genesis 1:27

"Scriptura est non in legendo, sed in intelligendo" ("Scripture not in words, but in understanding"), wrote the famous IV century theologian Hilary of Pictavia. And our understanding of biblical texts is influenced by the culture in which we were raised and our pseudo-scientific beliefs.

For the past 200 years, we have lived in a culture where the idea of two separate and complementary sexes seems like a primordial truth. Therefore, Genesis 1:27 is automatically understood as an affirmation of the binary nature of human sexuality.

For the past 200 years, we have lived in a culture where the idea of two separate and complementary sexes seems like a primordial truth. Therefore, Genesis 1:27 is automatically understood as an affirmation of the binary nature of human sexuality.

Of course, if any of us remembers the 17th century, he would say that the idea of two independent sexes is a modernist ingenuity of the Romantic era that destroys traditional values.

> "We say and believe that there are only two sexes, but even 150-200 years ago, it was believed that there was only one gender — male. And women were declared an insufficient man, that is, an anatomically imperfect copy of the male body, therefore weak, with various anomalies, so everything is presented to women "not as it should be". Arthur Schopenhauer wrote in 1851 that a woman is "like an intermediate stage between a child and a man, who is a real human". However, even after "discovering" the female sex, she was still always considered secondary, subordinate, dependent

> and, at the same time, hostile to the male." (D. Isaev. Deconstruction of the heteronormative matrix. — Translated from Russian)

Medieval commentators, being fascinated by Plato's dialectic, had their own unbiblical motives for seeing gender dualism in Genesis 1:27.

> "Saint Maxim discusses the special mission entrusted to man: since creation consists of several successive acts of division, man's primary task is to overcome these divisions by synthesizing them in an appropriate way.
>
> Since creation consisted of several successive divisions, the task of human life is to overcome these divisions in their respective syntheses. The most important division upon which the whole reality of created being rests is the division into created and uncreated... Next in importance is the division of the created world into heavenly and earthly, speculative and sensual nature. In sensual nature, heaven is separated from earth. A paradise is distinguished on the surface of the earth; the person living in paradise is divided into two genders — male and female. So Adam's vocation was to transcend all these divisions by his conscious work. Gradually overcoming these opposites, Adam had to lead all created things to the highest goal of existence — deification." (E. Hitruk. The ontological status of sex in Christian anthropology. — Translated from Russian)

However, the modern reader must either find that the Bible is contradicting scientifically established facts at this point, or else understand the Genesis 1:27 passage differently.

The New England Skeptical Society's professional medical website, Science-Based Medicine, states:

> "The notion that sex is not strictly binary is not even scientifically controversial. Among experts it is a given, an unavoidable conclusion derived from actually understanding the biology of sex. It is more accurate to describe biological sex in humans as bimodal, but not strictly binary. Bimodal means that there are essentially two dimensions to the continuum of biological sex. In order for sex to be binary there would need to be two non-overlapping and unambiguous ends to that continuum, but there clearly isn't. There is every conceivable type of overlap in the middle — hence bimodal, but not binary.... It is absolutely true that humans display sexual dimorphism, with a typical male and typical female set of traits. There is no third sex, or pole, or sexual archetype... Biological sex has only two poles, with one axis of variation between them..." (Dr. Steven Paul Novella. The Science of Biological Sex.)

Molecular biologist Liza Brusman notes:

> "The science is clear — sex is a spectrum. Yet the solution to the misunderstanding of sex doesn't end with scientists. We also need better public education and structural changes to recognize and protect people and their biology." (Liza Brusman. Sex isn't binary, and we should stop acting like it is.)

However, the reason is not only poor education, but also personal motivations to accept pseudo-scientific ideas. Our contemporaries, who believe in the flat Earth, studied in schools where it was clearly taught that the Earth is spherical.

It is significant that the phenomena of intersex are known in rabbinic literature. This means that medieval Jewish ideas about the nature of gender are closer to the modern bimodal model than to the binary model promoted by Christian fundamentalists. Although the social and religious norms of Judaism are known by two genders (as we would say now) — men and women — but various intersex people are encouraged to follow male gender norms in some cases and female norms in others.

> "Two sexes have never been enough to describe human variety. Not in biblical times and not now. Before we knew much about biology, we made social rules to administer sexual diversity. The ancient Jewish rabbinical code known as the Tosefta, for example, sometimes treated people who had male and female parts (such as testes and a vagina) as women — they could not inherit property or serve as priests; at other times, as men — forbidding them to shave or be secluded with women." (Dr. Anne Fausto-Sterling, Why Sex Is Not Binary)

Contemporary Rabbi David J. Meyer explains:

> "In fact, and strikingly, our Jewish legal tradition identifies no fewer than six distinct "genders", certainly assuming as normative the male and female, but including as well designations which we now refer to as "intersex" identities. To use the Hebrew terms: the androgynos, one who has both male and female characteristics, the tumtum, one whose biology is unclear, the aylonit, who identified as female at birth, but at puberty, develops male characteristics, and the saris, who appears as male at birth, but later takes on more typically female biology. I would suggest, based on the study of these legal texts that the Jewish understanding of gender is neither binary nor even a grid into which every person must be forced to fit. Rather, we see gender diversity as a spectrum, truly a rainbow of possibilities for reflecting the Image of God." (Rabbi David J. Meyer. What the Torah Teaches Us About Gender Fluidity and Transgender Justice)

The Genesis passage we are discussing can be very organically understood precisely in the spirit of the bi-modality, not the binary, of human sexuality. Here's what the Religious Action Center for Reform Judaism suggests:

> "We understand the verse, "male and female God created them" as a merism, a figure of speech in which a totality is expressed by two contrasting parts. This verse was interpreted as such by Rabbi Margaret Wenig. For example, "old and young", as the Prophet Joel foresees: "The old shall dream dreams, and the youth shall see visions." That is to say: old, young, and everyone in between. Similarly, "near and far," as in Isaiah's call: "Greetings of peace to those near and far." And those in between. So we learn that God created the human being as "male and female" — and every combination in between." (Ibid.)

This understanding of the passage is consistent not only with modern natural science, but also with the internal context. Merism occurs repeatedly in this chapter of Genesis.
"In the beginning, God created the heavens and the earth" (Genesis 1:1) orthodox arch-priest Alexander Men explains that the expression 'heaven and earth' "corresponds to the Sumerian 'ankhi', that is, the Universe". In the traditional interpretation of St. Basil the Great is also understood as "two extremes denoting the whole universe... Of course, if there is something between heaven and earth, it was created together with these extremes" (Orig.: Μέγας Βασηλίος. Ἡ Ἑξαήμερος Δημιουργία).
"And there was evening and morning, the first day" (Genesis 1:1). It is clear that a biblical day includes not only evening and morning, but in other parts of the 24-hour cycle. Merism is used here: the extreme positions of the sun (sunset and sunrise) are pointed out to indicate the entire diurnal cycle.

As we can see, the biblical account of the creation of man can be organically and coherently understood outside the binary paradigm. Therefore, the phrase "the creation of man and woman" does not prove that human nature is divided into two sexes whose boundaries are nowhere and never crossed.

This fact destroys all the subsequent logical chains of fundamentalists, who assert that both sexes complement and compensate each other, so that only in heterosexual relationships does a person acquire the fullness of nature and thus receive the opportunity for salvation. According to this logic, in a homosexual relationship people do not complete each other, nor can they attain the fullness of human nature and receive salvation. Therefore, supposedly, homosexual relationships are sinful and God-opposed.

However, if the absence of intercourse with the opposite sex leads to eternal damnation, could there have been single men among the apostles? How then could the virgin apostle Paul extol virginity as the highest way of spiritual life and recommend that it be chosen whenever possible?

> "Now concerning the things whereof ye wrote: It is good for a man not to touch a woman... Yet I would that all men were even as I myself. Howbeit each man hath his own gift from God, one after this manner, and another after that. But I say to the unmarried and to widows, It is good for them if they abide even as I." (1 Corinthians 7:1, 7-8)

Marriage of Adam and Eve — Genesis 2:23-24

The end of the second chapter of Genesis actually describes the marriage of Adam and Eve as a union of one man and one woman. But fundamentalists include in this section what is not there. The end of the second chapter of Genesis actually describes the marriage of Adam and Eve as a union of one man and one woman. But fundamentalists include in this section what is not there.

On the contrary, the following biblical account refutes this. Strictly speaking, Eve was a close biological relative of Adam (she was created from his rib, whatever that means). Some biblically righteous people also marry relatives and seem to follow the Adam and Eve marriage formula. Sarah was Abraham's sister by her father's side. Isaac married his third cousin (Genesis 24:15; 67), and Jacob married his second cousin (Genesis 29:3; 28). However, incest is already forbidden as a sin already in the Law of Moses (Leviticus 18:1-30; Deuteronomy 27:20, 22, 23). Almost all Christian churches consider consanguineous marriage to be sinful. The Eastern Church and the Roman Catholic Church prohibit marriages up to and including the fourth degree of consanguinity.

If you, as a Christian, believe that consanguineous marriages are sinful and impermissible, then you cannot point to the marriage of Adam and Eve as an example of the only human union ever permissible!

Monogamy is also not an easy task. While married to Sarah, Abraham had sexual relations with his concubine Hagar. After Sarah's death, he entered into a second marriage with Hittur. Jacob was married to Leah and Rachel at the same time. At the same time, he had children from their maids, Bilhah and Zilpah. The holy kings David and Solomon had dozens of wives and concubines.

In the Book of Numbers (1:12), Miriam and Aaron reproached Moses for marrying a foreigner, an Ethiopian, even before Zipporah.

> "Tharbis was the daughter of the king of the Ethiopians: she happened to see Moses as he led the army near the walls, and fought with great courage; and admiring the subtility of his undertakings, and believing him to be the author of the Egyptians' success, when they had before despaired of recovering their liberty, and to be the occasion of the great danger the Ethiopians were in, when they had before boasted of their great achievements, she fell deeply in love with him; and upon the prevalency of that passion, sent to him the most faithful of all her servants to discourse with him about their marriage. He thereupon accepted the offer, on condition she would procure the delivering up of the city; and gave her the assurance of an oath to take her to his wife; and that when he had once taken possession of the city, he would not break his oath to her. No sooner was the agreement made, but it took effect immediately; and when Moses had cut off the Ethiopians, he gave thanks to God, and consummated his marriage, and led the Egyptians back to their own land." (Flavius Josephus. Antiquities of the Jews, Book II. — Translation by William Whiston.)

According to this story, God does not punish Moses with leprosy, but Miriam.

The rules of inheritance in Deuteronomy equalize the rights of the children of a beloved and an unloved wife. This shows that in the Law of Moses, marriage to both wives is equally legal and equally approved by God.

> "If a man have two wives, the one beloved, and the other hated, and they have borne him children, both the beloved

> and the hated; and if the first-born son be hers that was hated; then it shall be, in the day that he causeth his sons to inherit that which he hath, that he may not make the son of the beloved the first-born before the son of the hated, who is the first-born: but he shall acknowledge the first-born, the son of the hated, by giving him a double portion of all that he hath; for he is the beginning of his strength; the right of the first-born is his." (Deuteronomy 21:15-17)

Interestingly, there is no direct prohibition of polygamy throughout the Bible. Although there are phrases in the New Testament that make monogamy a higher example of virtue.

> "A bishop then must be blameless, the husband of one wife, vigilant, sober, of good behaviour, given to hospitality, apt to teach." (1 Timothy 3:2)

> "Let the deacons be the husbands of one wife, ruling their children and their own houses well." (1 Timothy 3:12)

> "If any be blameless, the husband of one wife, having fathful children not accused of riot or unruly." (Titus 1:6)

Many researchers believe that the Church strongly opposed polygamy due to pressure from Roman law. Although not immediately.

> "It is of indisputed historic record that both the Christian Church and the Christian State in different centuries and under a number of differing circumstances gave their influence in favor of polygamy. The Roman emperor, Valentinian I., in the fourth century, authorized christians to take two wives; in the eighth century the great Charlemagne holding power over both church and state, in his own person practiced polygamy, having six, or according to some

> authorities, nine wives. With the Reformation this system entered Protestantism. As the first synod in North America was called for the purpose of trying a woman for heresy, so the first synod of the reformation was assembled for the purpose of sustaining polygamy, thus farther debasing woman in the marital relation. The great German reformer, Luther, although perhaps himself free from the lasciviousness of the old priesthood was not strictly monogamic in principle. When applied to by Philip, Landgrave of Hesse Cassel, for permission to marry a second wife while his first wife, Margaret of Savoy, was still living, he called together a synod of six of the principal reformers — Melancthon and Bucer among them — who in joint consultation decided "that as the Bible nowhere condemns polygamy, and as it has been invariably practiced by the highest dignitaries of the church," such marriage was legitimate, and the required permission was given. Luther himself with both the Old and the New Testaments in hand, saying, "I confess for my part that if a man wishes to marry two or more wives, I cannot forbid him, nor is his conduct ant to the Holy Scriptures." (Matilda Joslyn Gage. Woman, Church and state, Chapter VII. Polygamy.)

Among other historically changed circumstances of the marriage of Adam and Eve, we see that it was not certified by authorized representatives from the Church or from the state (society). According to modern church and secular legal criteria, their union is not a legal marriage, but cohabitation.

Thus, in the example of the union of Adam and Eve, there are too many circumstances that did not and are not fulfilled in the marriages that the Bible writes about and that are recognized by modern Christian Churches. Therefore, the heterosexuality nature of this union is as obligatory a feature of all subsequent marriages as is incest and the absence of a representative of the Church or State in the marriage.

The only thing fundamentalists might object to is that heterosexual marriage is at least favorably mentioned in the Bible, while homosexual marriage is not. Therefore, we know for sure that the first is pleasing to God. But we cannot say the same about the second one.

The answer must be that the Bible also does not condemn gay marriage. Therefore, we cannot conclude from the Bible that God condemns such unions.

Once, in response to the argument that throughout the history of the Church, marriage had always been the union of a man and a woman, an opponent wittily observed that for many centuries of human history, elections were held only between men and the state, without the participation of women. The question is, do Christians have the right to be creative in their lives and practice customs and traditions that are not expressly prescribed by the Bible? Which of the two possible principles does the Bible itself proclaim: "whatever is not permitted is forbidden" or "whatever is not forbidden is permitted"? The New Testament testifies to the principle of freedom: Christians are allowed to do everything except that which is harmful to spiritual health, except sin.

> "All things are lawful unto me, but all things are not expedient: all things are lawful for me, but I will not be brought under the power of any." (1 Corinthians 6:12)

> "All things are lawful for me, but all things are not expedient: all things are lawful for me, but all things edify not!" (1 Corinthians 10:23)

This principle even worked in the Old Testament. The ninth chapter of the book of Esther tells how the Jews instituted Purim without God's direction. The Bible nowhere condemns such an initiative. The Book of

Esther is one of the canonical books of the Bible. And Jews celebrate Purim to this day.

Thus, if we do not find anything dangerous to spiritual health in same-sex love relationships (that is, if we understand that they do not take away the ability to love faithfully and sacrificially), then we have every right to reconsider what we call the institution of marriage, taking into account new needs, arising from a new cultural and historical context and new scientific knowledge.

The Sin of Sodom — Genesis 19

Genesis 19 tells how God punished the people of Sodom (and the surrounding cities) for their rampant wickedness. Due to various historical misunderstandings, which there is no point in discussing now, fundamentalists are convinced that the inhabitants of Sodom were punished for homosexuality. In church jargon, homosexuality is often called the sin of Sodom, sodomy.

Surprisingly, in the Scriptures that speak of the destruction of Sodom, there is not a single word about homosexuality or homosexual practices. In the biblical story there is an episode when the inhabitants of Sodom want to sexually rape Lot's guests (angels in the form of young men). But, firstly, in this crime, as the Septuagint says (19:4), ἅπας ὁ λαός - the whole people. This means that there were women among the participants. Consequently, the attack was not homosexual, but bisexual in nature. Second, sexually assaulting a guest is a grave sin and crime, whether it is homosexual or heterosexual assault.

Nowhere in the Bible does it state that God condemned the people of Sodom because of their homosexuality. The prophets, explaining what the Sodomites were guilty of, list completely different sins:

> "Behold, this was the iniquity of thy sister Sodom, pride, fulness of bread, and abundance of idleness was in her and in her daughters, neither did she strengthen the hand of the poor and needy. And they were haughty, and committed abomination before me: therefore I took them away as I saw good." (Ezekiel 16:49-50)

> "Hear this word, ye kine of Bashan, that are in the mountain of Samaria, which oppress the poor, which crush the needy, which say to their masters, Bring, and let us drink <...> I have overthrown some of you, as God overthrew Sodom and Gomorrah, and ye were as a firebrand plucked out of the burning: yet have ye not returned unto me, saith the Lord." (Amos 4:1,11)

Moses predicted disasters like the destruction of Sodom and Gomorrah. However, he pointed out that the reason for the punishment was not homosexuality, but spiritual fornication - idolatry (Deuteronomy 29:22-26).

In the New Testament, Jesus mentions Sodom and Gomorrah when speaking about inhospitably. He compares these cities to those that refused hospitality to His apostles:

> "And whoever has neither received you, nor listened to your words, departing from that house or city, shake off the dust from your feet. Amen I say to you, it will be more tolerable for the land of Sodom and Gomorrah in the day of judgment, than for that city." (Matthew 10:14-15)

In Jewish tradition, Sodom and Gomorrah were also associated with arrogance, greed, disrespect for the poor, and xenophobia. The 1st century Jewish historian Josephus writes:

> "About this time the Sodomites grew proud, on account of their riches and great wealth; they became unjust towards men, and impious towards God, insomuch that they did not call to mind the advantages they received from him: they hated strangers, and abused themselves with Sodomitical practices. God was therefore much displeased at them, and determined to punish them for their pride, and to overthrow

> their city, and to lay waste their country, until there should neither plant nor fruit grow out of it." (Flavius Josephus. Antiquities of the Jews, Book II. — Translation by William Whiston.)

Sometimes fundamentalists go as far as outright falsification and say that Josephus considered homosexuality to be a sin of sodomy. The following passage from "Antiquities of the Jews" is quoted in support of this statement:

> "Now when the Sodomites saw the young men to be of beautiful countenances, and this to an extraordinary degree, and that they took up their lodgings with Lot, they resolved themselves to enjoy these beautiful boys by force and violence." (Ibid.)

It is clear that the author focuses on the hospitality of Lot and Abraham, which he contrasts with the behavior of the Sodomites. There is no indication in the text that Josephus condemned homosexual interest in young men. The author describes their desire to rape guests with a negative epithet. Isn't sexual abuse a sin if it is heterosexual in nature!
The Babylonian Talmud supports this view:

> "The people of Sodom said: Since we live in a land from which bread comes and has the dust of gold, we have everything that we need. Why do we need travelers, as they come only to divest us of our property? Come, let us cause the proper treatment of travelers to be forgotten from our land, as it is stated: "He breaks open a watercourse in a place far from inhabitants, forgotten by pedestrians, they are dried up, they have moved away from men" (Job 28:4)." (Babylonian Talmud: Tractate Sanhedrin. — Translated by Rabbi Adin Steinsaltz Even-Israel.)

The logic of the biblical story also contrasts the xenophobia of the Sodomites with the hospitality of Abraham and Lot.
From the apostle Paul's hint we see that the story of Genesis 19 is primarily a story of hospitality for him.

> "And do not be willing to forget hospitality. For by it, certain persons, without realizing it, have received Angels as guests." (Hebrews 13:2)

However, homonegativists are not discouraged and offer to prove that the sin of the inhabitants of Sodom was homosexuality, quoting the Epistle of Jude:

> "And also Sodom and Gomorrah, and the adjoining cities, in similar ways, having given themselves over to fornication and to the pursuing of other flesh, were made an example, suffering the punishment of eternal fire." (Jude 1:7)

Proponents of a homophobic interpretation of this passage claim that the expression "pursuing of other flesh" is a euphemism for homosexuality. It is logical to ask: "Why?" They do not have any positive arguments to support such an understanding. There is only the counter question: "What, if not homosexuality, does this mean?"
In fact, biblical scholars disagree on exactly how to understand this passage. It just seems that this expression is a certain stable figure of speech. However, we will not actually find it in other literature of the time. The Greek expression 'σαρκὸς ἑτέρας' [sarkos hetheras] is inappropriate to express same-sex sexual attraction. 'Hetheras' here means another, different. The same word is part of the Greek term heterosexuality. The essence of homosexuality is the opposite: to seek not another body, but the same body. This term is also of Greek origin. However, it uses another Greek word that is an antonym of ἕτερος: ὁμός [homos] — equal, similar, the same.

Fundamentalists explain that "another body" means "not this body": not the body that is intended for this person. However, this understanding also applies to the sin of cheating on one's wife and even to the sin of bestiality. Thus, the only reason homonegatives see the phrase "pursuing of other flesh" as describing homosexuality is because they long for it to be that way.

The most honest homonegativists have long recognized that the story of Sodom is not suitable for condemning homosexuality. This is what the famous contemporary Bible scholar Richard B. Hayes writes in a book that was named by the evangelical Christian online magazine Christianity Today as one of the 100 most important of the 20th century religious books:

> "The notorious story of Sodom and Gomorrah — often cited in connection with homosexuality — is actually irrelevant to the topic. The "men of Sodom" come pounding on Lot's door, apparently with the intention of gang-raping Lot's two visitor — who, as we readers know, are actually angels... The gang-rape scenario exemplifies the wickedness of the city, but there is nothing in the passage pertinent to a judgment about the morality of consensual homosexual intercourse. Indeed, there is nothing in the rest of the biblical tradition, save an obscure reference in Jude 7, to suggest that the sin of Sodom was particularly identified with sexual misconduct of any kind." (Richard B. Hays. Moral Vision of the New Testament.)

Despite the fact that the author himself considers homosexuality a sin, regarding the Epistle of Jude he adds:

> "According to Jude 7, "Sodom and Gomorrah and the surrounding cities, which, in the same manner as they, indulged in sexual immorality and went after other flesh, serve

as an example by undergoing a punishment of eternal fire". The phrase "went after other flesh" (apelthousai opis sarkos heteras) refers to their pursuit of nonhuman (i.e., angelic!) "flesh". The expression sarkos heteras means "flesh of another kind"; thus, it is impossible to construe this passage as a condemnation of homosexual desire, which entails precisely the pursuit of flesh of the same kind." (Ibid.)

"Shalt not lie with mankind, as with womankind" — Leviticus 18:22; 20:13

> "Thou shalt not lie with mankind, as with womankind: it is abomination." (Leviticus 18:22)

> "And if a man lie with mankind, as with womankind, both of them have committed abomination..." (Leviticus 20:13)

In many cases, queer-theologians show that the cultural and historical context of these verses points to the homosexual acts used by the Canaanites in idolatrous orgies. In other words, in those lines, the author is not dealing with cases where homosexual partners love each other and build strong, lasting relationships.

I will show two more reasons why it is very difficult to see the condemnation of homosexuality in the Book of Leviticus.

The first reason is that in ancient culture, women were considered inferior. And because of this, both sexes are expected to behave in a certain way in society and in bed. We already talked about this in the chapter: "Why the Bible doesn't talk about homosexuality." If you read the text in the light of this feature of the ancient mentality, it becomes clear that "you cannot lie with a man as with a woman" only means that during a homosexual act, a man should not allow himself and his partner to play a "feminine" passive role. This understanding is one of the interpretation options in the rabbinic tradition.

> "And Shmuel holds: It is written: "And you shall not lie with a male as with a woman," indicating that the halakha of a male who engages in intercourse passively is like that of a woman;

> just as the intercourse of a woman has the halakhic status of intercourse from when she is three years old, the same is true with regard to a male who engages in intercourse passively. Consequently, in Shmuel's opinion, one who engages in intercourse with a male who is older than three is liable." (Babylonian Talmud: Tractate Sanhedrin. — Translated by Rabbi Adin Steinsaltz Even-Israel.)

Stephen J. Patterson, professor of religious and ethical studies at Willamette University, offers three options to sum up what it meant in the Ancient East to "lie with a man as with a woman":

> "What did it mean for "a man to lie with a man as with a woman" in the Ancient Near East? Male-male same-gendered sex in the Ancient Near East — so far as ancient texts discuss it — had three possible meanings: domination, recreation, and religious devotion... What meaning, then, did the sex acts referred to in Leviticus have? Theoretically it could have been any of the three: domination, recreation, or religious devotion." (Stephen Patterson. When a Man Lies with a Man as with a Woman.)

I think it goes without saying that it is not acceptable for Jews to demonstrate their superiority by humiliating subordinates or captives with sexual violence. It is also unthinkable that a worshiper of one God would participate in idolatrous orgies.
Patterson points out that male-male sex for entertainment was similar to sex to demonstrate superiority:

> "Ancient Near Eastern recreational male-male sex was a similar thing. This is something one might do with a slave or personal servant in the absence of female companionship. It was also frowned upon in some cultures, who viewed it as

> exploitative and demeaning to the man or boy who was forced to play the role of "woman" in such sexual activity (note the inherent sexism). To lie with a man "as with a woman" pretty much captures the point. Men were supposed to be men, not women. Men pitch; they don't catch." (Ibid.)

The researcher draws attention to an important feature:

> "None of these meanings depended upon the homosexuality of the participants. In fact, it is quite the opposite. All depended on the assumption that the initiator of the act was acting in the very heterosexual role of male. A man could dominate another man by buggering him, thus forcing him into the subordinate role of female. That is why it is permitted to rape one's enemies at the end of a battle, but not to bugger one's slave. In the first, violent aggression is part of what the soldier signs on for. In the second, you're just taking advantage. In the case of ritual sex, the devotee is seen as performing the heterosexual male role of planting his seed in another, in this case a man re-imagined as part-female. So, was there actual gay sex in the Ancient Near East? Probably. But it is never discussed in the surviving literature." (Ibid.)

So whatever the authors of Leviticus had in mind, they certainly weren't writing about homosexual love in the modern sense. The scholar acknowledges that modern biblical scholarship presents different versions of what these passages specifically forbid. But more than a decade ago, Bible scholars discovered exactly what this passage could not mean.

> "But we can say very clearly what it does not mean. It does not mean don't fall in love with another man and have intimate sexual relations with him. Male-male sex just did not have

> that connotation in the Ancient Near East... Male-male sex in the Ancient Near East does not mean "I love you." It means "I own you." Today, of course, it is different. Male-male sex can mean "I love you." To such a thing Leviticus offers no comment." (Ibid.)

The second reason that prevents these verses from being considered as prohibiting homosexual relations is the Jewish tradition of translating and understanding these verses. Let's give a word to the Russian biblical scholar Dmitry Shchedrovichi:

> "The original says: [ve-et-zahar lo tishkav mishkavei isha].
>
> This can be translated twofold: "And don't lie with a man who has women's beds", or "And do not lie with a man in the beds of women".
>
> According to some interpreters, this refers to a man — [zahar], possessing by nature two "beds", like a woman — [isha] (because in the phrase [mishkevei isha], "a woman's bed", the plural is used). Therefore, we are talking about a hermaphrodite (i.e. a person who has both male and female sexual characteristics). In a number of pagan religions, including Canaanite, hermaphrodites were considered to be the chosen ones of the gods, they had a special role in the cult, often they became priests. Since a hermaphrodite, after assuming the female role and conceiving, is in most cases unable to bear and bear a child, the commandment requires him to play the male role in marriage. This is why the hermaphrodite is referred to in the verse above [zachar] as "man".

> According to other interpreters, in this verse the Torah forbids simultaneous (group) or alternating coitus between two men and one woman, which could lead to the conception of a child. Such conception (taking place during ritual orgies) was widespread among the Canaanites and was even considered especially favorable for them: children born from such coitus were considered "children of the gods" and often became priests, rulers, etc. <...>
>
> Thus, Scripture does not contain any general prohibitive or permissive injunctions against homosexual relationships — any injunctions in this regard are derived from some other, usually confessional or sociocultural, but not biblical, view." (Dmitry Shchedrovitsky. Introduction to the Old Testament. — Translation from Russian.)

The famous 12th century rabbi Abraham ibn Ezra, interpreting Leviticus 18:22, expresses the first tradition:

> "Rabbi Hananel, his memory is blessed, said that there is someone who creates anew in his body the likeness of female flesh, which he did not have at birth; and some say it means androgynous; and all these definitions are related to the fact that the expression "mishkevei isha" ("woman's beds") here is in the plural, i.e. it refers to one male person with two "beds."

The College of Jewish Theologians, which prepared the Greek translation of the Septuagint, saw here the prohibition of group sex. This is how Shchedrovicki explains it in his answer to one of the critics.

> "The Septuagint verse of Leviticus 18:22 reads: 'Kai meta ãrsenos u koimatese koiten gunaikos' — 'And you shall not lie with a man on a woman's bed.' The Greek 'meta' next to

> the genitive case means exactly 'together'. And 'gunaikas' are definitely 'feminine' and not 'masculine'. So the translators of the Septuagint chose from these two variants of understanding the one that refers to the intimacy of two or more men with a woman at the same time."

Another nuance is which Hebrew word is translated as 'abomination': 'toebah' or 'to'eva'. This word has a very subtle connotation that is not easy to identify, because sometimes it refers to idolatrous traditions, sometimes to requirements of ritual impurity, and sometimes to what seems to us to be natural moral norms because we were brought up in a society where this is the norm. Although it did not seem so to the neighbors of ancient Israel.

Jay Michaelson, Ph.D. from Yale University and Doctor of Jewish Thought from the Hebrew University of Jerusalem, analyzed the use of the word toeva in the Torah to determine its true meaning. He came to this conclusion:

> "The word "abomination" is found, of course, in the King James translation of Leviticus 18:22... Yet this is a thoroughly misleading rendition of the word toevah... Yet a close reading of the term toevah suggests an entirely different meaning: something permitted to one group, and forbidden to another. Though there is (probably) no etymological relationship, toevah means taboo". (Dr. Jay Michaelson. Does the bible really call homosexuality an "abomination"?)

The researcher draws attention to:

> "Deut. 12:31, 13:14, 17:4, 27:15, and 32:16 further identify idolatry, child sacrifice, witchcraft, and other "foreign" practices as toevah, and Deut. 20:18 says that avoiding toevah justifies the genocide of the Hittites, Amorites, Canaanaites,

> Perizzites, Hivites, and Jebusites. So, toevah is serious, but it is serious as a particular class of cultic offense: a transgression of national boundary. It is certainly not "abomination."
>
> Toevah is used four times in Leviticus 18—once to refer to male homosexual acts, and then three times as an umbrella term. As in Deuteronomy, the signal feature of toevot is that the other nations of the Land of Israel do them: "You shall therefore keep my statutes and my judgments, and shall not commit these toevot... because the people who were in the land before you did these toevot and made the land impure (tameh)" (Lev. 18:26-27; see also Lev. 18:29)." (Ibid.)

A similar conclusion regarding the use of the term in the historical books of the Old Testament:

> "In all these cases, toevah refers to a foreign cultic behavior wrongly practiced by Israelites and Israelite kings." (Ibid.)

In the prophetic corpus toeva is associated with idolatry:

> "In one extended passage (Ez. 8:1-18), Ezekiel is taken on a visionary tour of toevot, all of which have to do with idolatry... This extended passage, with six mentions of toevah, links the term in every instance with avodah zara, or idolatry.
>
> In five instances, Ezekiel mentions toevah together with both idolatry and zimah or znut, "whoredom" (Ez. 16:22, 16:36, 16:58, 23:26, 43:8), strongly suggesting that the nature of sexual toevah is not mere lewdness, and certainly not loving intimate expression, but sexuality in a cultic context." (Ibid.)

But the evidence that toeva is not something inherently bad, ontologically, is found in the book of Genesis.

> "Genesis 43:32 states that eating with Israelites is toevah for Egyptians. Gen. 43:34 states that shepherds are toevah to Egyptians—the sons of Israel are themselves shepherds. In Exodus 8:22, Moses describes Israelite sacrifices as being toevat mitzrayim (toevah of Egypt), although obviously Israelite ritual is not an objective "abomination." If toevah means abomination, then eating with shepherds, eating with Israelites, and Israelite sacrifices themselves must be abominable! Since this clearly is not the case, toevah cannot mean "abomination" in any ontological sense—it must be a relative quality." (Ibid.)

The author insists:

> "Now, if by "abomination," the King James means a cultural prohibition—something which a particular culture abhors but another culture enjoys—then the term makes sense. But in common parlance, the term has come to mean much more than that. Today, it connotes something horrible, something contrary to the order of nature itself, or God's plan, or the institution of the family, or whatever... In fact, toevah is mostly about idolatry, and male homosexual behavior is only as abominable as remarriage or not keeping kosher. Whenever we use the word "abomination" we are perpetuating the misunderstanding of biblical text and the religious persecution of LGBT people... Personally, I like "taboo" as a replacement. It conveys the culturally relative nature of toevah, has some connotation of foreignness, and rightly aligns the taboo against homosexuality with taboos against, for example, eating unkosher food. It also has a vaguely archaic feel, which it should... Alternatively, we could stick with the Hebrew term, the foreignness of which heightens the foreignness of the biblical concerns about homosexuality.)

> One thing remains clear, though: what's really abominable here is the word "abomination" itself." (Ibid.)

This implication is also supported by the fact that the toeva we are discussing is located in that part of the Book of Leviticus called the "Code of Holiness." This code deals specifically with the rules by which the people of God are to be distinguished from idolatrous nations.

> "Do not do as the Egyptians did, among whom you lived, and do not follow the customs of the land of Canaan, into which I will bring you, do not walk in their statutes." (Leviticus 18:3)

> "And ye shall not walk in the customs of the nation, which I cast out before you: for they did all these things, and therefore I abhorred them... I am Jehovah your God, who hath separated you from the peoples." (Leviticus 20:23-24)

Meanwhile, many provisions of the "Code of Holiness" are not relevant for Christians.

> "But Peter answered, 'By no means, Lord!' I have never eaten anything tainted or unclean" The voice said a second time: "What God has cleansed, do not call defiled!" (Acts 10:14-15)

Therefore, additional arguments are needed to insist that certain taboos of the "Code of Holiness" are still in effect. In other words, the prohibition in question seems to apply to idolatrous orgies. However, gay Christians do not intend to use their sexuality to worship idols. Therefore, there is no reason to use these passages against them.

Rev. Roger Farnworth, an Anglican scholar who studies the philological features of Ecclesiastes 18:22 and 20:13 and their translations, concludes:

> "There is a lack of clarity in the original Hebrew which has then been compounded by the choices made by translators. The net effect of these two factors is that two texts which are complex in their original form, have been rendered simply in English and have then been built on by others in a way that the original Hebrew probably does not warrant." (Roger Farnworth. Leviticus 18:22 and Leviticus 20:13.)

All this inevitably leads to the conclusion that the verses of Leviticus 18:22 and 20:13 are not at all as clear as they first appeared to us. There are many reasons why they do not apply to modern homosexual love relationships. They are not suitable for proving Biblical homonegativity.

Arsenokoitai and Malakoi — 1 Corinthians 6:9; 1 Timothy 1:10

The term "homosexual" first appeared in 1868 in a letter in German by the Austro-Hungarian publicist and politician Karl Maria Kertbeny. In English, this word began to be used only in the nineties of the 19th century. Around the same time, the first signs appeared that homosexuality was gradually beginning to be recognized as a separate sexual orientation characteristic of a certain segment of society. The concept of the existence of sexual orientation is also a product of the modern era.

Therefore, the authors of some modern Bible translations made a very bold decision by adding a modern concept to the ancient text:

> "Or do you not know that the unrighteous will not inherit the kingdom of God? Do not be deceived; neither fornicators, nor idolaters, nor adulterers, nor [a]effeminate, nor homosexuals, 10 nor thieves, nor the covetous, nor drunkards, nor revilers, nor swindlers, will inherit the kingdom of God. ." (1 Corinthians 6:9-10)

He showed the same determination elsewhere:

> "...for those involved in sexual immorality, for homosexuals, for kidnappers, for liars, for false witnesses, and for whatever else goes against the healthy teaching..." (1 Timothy 1:9-10; New American Standard Bible)

The word "homosexual" first appeared in the 1946 English translation of the Bible.

In our case, the author translated 'homosexuals' two Greek words (from 1 Corinthians 6:9): ἀρσενοκοίτης [arsenokoites] and μαλακος [malakos]. For comparison, let us remember that in the translation of 1557, arsenocoites are translated as 'bugger', in the translation of 1885 — 'abusers of themselves with mankind'. As you can see, previous translators did not agree on the meaning of this word. They had to guess about its true meaning.

One method that is still used by some is guessing the meaning by etymology. The starting point in this case is the fact that the Apostle Paul's neologism 'aresenokoites' consists of two Greek lexemes: 'arsen', which means 'man', and 'coites', which means 'bed' in the sense of sleeping with someone.

However, firstly, etymology does not always reflect the meaning of a word. For example, the English word "butterfly" is etymologically derived from the words "butter" and "fly". But some linguist from the future will not be able to restore the true meaning of a word only on the basis of knowledge of these parts.

Secondly, in this case, based on etymology, we can draw conclusions about different meanings: one who goes to bed with a man; a man with whom someone goes into bed. And these are just the possible literal meanings. However, behind these meanings there may be various social phenomena: male prostitution, cohabitation of a man with another male donor or female donor, etc.

Typically, the meaning of ancient words can be understood from the context in which they are used. However, the term arsenocoites is a neologism, a word coined by the Apostle Paul. Before him, this word had not appeared in literature. After that, it usually occurs without enough context to explain the meaning. This gives homonegativists the freedom to give the word a meaning that suits them. Although they have to

hypothesize why Paul came up with his own word for homosexual relations when the Greek language had enough of its own words for it.
According to one version, Paul wanted to make a hidden reference to the Greek translation of Leviticus 20:13, where arsenos and koite appear next to each other and form a similar-sounding phrase. However, we have already established that the prohibitions of the book of Leviticus do not apply to homosexual love relationships. So, if Paul is referring here to the Book of Leviticus, by arsenokoites he is not referring to homosexuals as such.
Medieval translators could also only guessed at the true meaning of the apostle's neologism. The medieval Latin translation of the Bible, the Vulgate Clementina, translates ἀρσενοκοίτης as 'masculorum concubitoribus' meaning concubinage or pimping. Martin Luther in 1545 the translation uses the word 'Knabenschänder' (boy molester) and hints at pedophilia.
Likewise, translators make different assumptions about the meaning of Paul's word μαλακος. Literally, it means "soft". Jesus Christ uses this word in Matthew 11:8 and Luke 7:25, referring to the soft clothing worn by rich people accustomed to luxury. Obviously, this is a metaphor. But for whom?
Homonegativists believe that malakos is the lower, passive partner in the homosexual act, and arsenokoit is the upper, active partner. However, such a hypothesis is no more provable than many alternative translations.
Clement of Alexandria (2nd century) associates the word malakos with the effeminacy of rich men who care about their appearance. He says nothing about their sexual preferences. He simply emphasizes that such men become vulgar and provocative in their appearance, as is characteristic of harlots and prostitutes (The Paedagogus. Book III, Chapter 3. Against Men Who Embellish Themselves).
English philologist and theologian William Tyndale in 1526 In the Bible translation, this word was translated 'malakoi' as 'weaklings': someone who is weak in character. Martin Luther in 1534 the translation of this

word has a similar meaning: 'die Weichlinge'. 1560 In the Geneva Bible, malachions are called 'wantons'. According to 1611 In the King James Version, this term means 'effeminate': effeminate men. Many translations assume that the apostle is talking about male prostitution: New American Bible (1970), New International Version (1973), New Century (1987), New Revised Standard Version (1989), New Living Translation (1996), International Standard Version (2000), World English Bible (2005).

If we turn to those rare early texts that provide some context to explain the meaning of arsenokoitia, they will disappoint the homonegativists. They imply interspecies (angels, pagan gods, animals with humans) sex, or sex without conception (oral, anal, etc.). All this in ancient times was considered an unnatural sexual manifestation. However, the fact that arsenokoity cannot be identified with homosexual sexual relations is proven by the use of this word in the treatise "Repentance", which is attributed to the Patriarch of Constantinople John the Faster, canonized by the Eastern and Western Churches. Discussing the sin of incest, he writes:

> "Some even do this with their own mothers, while others do it with their adopted sisters or goddaughters. Thus, many men even commit the sin of arsenokoity with their women."

In the "Nomocanon" (Rule 7) of John the Faster we find another evidence of heterosexual arsenocoitia:

> "There is also female arsenokoitia, in which husbands, darkened and blinded by the enemy, abandoning natural affairs, fornicate in the anus with unfortunate women and sometimes with their wives."

Obviously, the sin of arsenokoity can also be committed during heterosexual intercourse. Thus, when we condemn arsenokoites, we do not condemn homosexuality as such. The Byzantine astrologer Rhetorius of Egypt (7th century) also wrote about heterosexual arsenokoites. He uses the expression: "arsenocoites and rapists of women."

No one knows exactly what the apostle Paul meant, but in medieval literature arsenokoitia probably meant penetration into the anus, regardless of the gender or sexual orientation of the participants in the sexual act.

Such sexual practices were considered unnatural because the use of the genitals could not lead to conception, not because it involved same-sex relationships. Of course, if two men were involved, one of them was unconsciously playing the role of passive recipient. And such a role, according to archaic ideas, was suitable only for a woman. Because women were considered inferior beings. This was considered the same sin as heterosexual sexual intercourse with a woman in an active position on top. But these superstitious beliefs of archaic culture do not care whether the sexual act is homosexual or heterosexual.

So every honest researcher, whatever hypothesis about the meaning of the word arsenokoites seems to him personally the most likely, must, following New #Testament scholar Professor Dale Martin of Yale University, say:

> "I should be clear about my claims here. I am not claiming to know what arsenokoités meant, I am claiming that no one knows what it meant." (Dale Martin, professor. Sex and the Single Savior: Gender and Sexuality in Biblical Interpretation)

The same is the case with the 'malakoi' metaphor.

“Against nature” — Romans 1:26-27

Pink, high heels, cheerleading, stockings. In our culture, these words are still mainly associated with the image of a woman.

But even before World War II, pink was considered a masculine color. It is a shade of red (the color of activity and strength).

Long before stockings entered the women's wardrobe, cropped stockings with suspenders were popular among men. Medieval men wore stockings while riding on horseback and with high heels. The latter were also considered an attribute of a man's wardrobe. They emphasized the higher position of men in society. If a woman dared to wear high heels, she was defying standards of decency and public morality.

Originally, cheerleading was a prestigious male sport. It was considered too difficult for girls. The cheerleaders were Eisenhower, Roosevelt and Reagan.

The purpose of this little excursion into history is to show how quickly society's understanding of what is normal, decent and natural is changing. And how much depends not on the natural nature of things, but on cultural prejudices.

If a modern reader were to read a magazine from 1918 that reprimanded some men for wearing feminine colors in violation of the norms of decency, he would probably think that those men were dressing in the style of pink Barbies. However, the author of the article at the beginning of the 20th century understood feminine colors as shades of blue.

The modern reader is misled by the phrase of the Apostle Paul about the sexual practices of the pagans, which are “against nature.” Homosexuality is often described by homonegativists as something contrary to nature. Therefore, it seems to them that the Apostle Paul meant the same thing. However, the views of the apostle and his contemporaries on the nature of human sexuality were very different from ours. They knew nothing about sexual orientation. Their moral criteria for evaluating sexual actions did not include the categories of homo- and hetero-.

> "Ancient categories of sexual experience differed considerably from our own... The central distinction in sexual morality was the distinction between active and passive roles. The gender of the object ... is not in itself morally problematic. Boys and women are very often treated interchangeably as objects of [male] desire. What is socially important is to penetrate rather than to be penetrated. Sex is understood fundamentally not as interaction, but as a doing of some thing to someone..." (Martha Nussbaum. The Bondage and Freedom of Eros.)

Let's try to re-read the apostle Paul through the eyes of his contemporaries.

> "For this reason, God gave them over to shameful passions, because their women also changed the relationship that is natural to the physical nature for that which is contrary to the physical nature; in the same way also men, leaving the physical natural intercourse with women, became inflamed in their desire for one another, men with men doing what is worthy of shame, and receiving in themselves the necessary recompense for their transgression." (Romans 1:26-27)

A literal translation of the Greek text that rebukes women is: *"females did change the natural use into that against nature."* The text does not specify what it was against nature that women began to use.
The Greek text says of men: *"likewise and men, abandoned the natural use of women, become excited in their pursuit for one another, men committing ugliness on men and receiving a reward corresponding to their error in themselves."*

If we understand what the Greek expressions "fisikēn chrēsin" (natural use) and "para fizikēn chrēsin" (above natural or against nature use) mean, we get a clue to the true meaning of the text.
The second-century writer Clement of Alexandria, following Jewish tradition, states that "unlawful for a man to have coitus without the purpose of procreation a man is forbidden to engage in sexual intercourse without the purpose of procreation." He elaborates his point:

> "Nature, both in regard to food and in regard to lawful marriage, allows only what is natural, expedient, and decent to be used. It permits the passionate desire to produce children. But all excesses and immoderatenesses are already against the laws of nature; those who allow them harm themselves by unnatural ties. First of all, hence the law that we should never sleep with young men as if with women... Except for your own wife" (Lev. 18, 20); only with her do you have the right to indulge in carnal pleasures in order to conceive a legitimate offspring; only this is allowed by the Logos. For those who, by what they do themselves, contribute to the creative activity of the Logos, the seed will not be rejected and will not do any harm, but it should not be sown on the horns of a bull." (Clemens of Alexandria. Pedagogue. Book 2)

The thought of Clement of Alexandria is similar to the Apostle Paul's statement. He even explains the reckoning to which men who practice "use against nature" condemn themselves.

> "So, a person loses vitality from ejaculation as much as he is a bodily organism, because at the beginning of life lies exactly what is connected with the end; therefore, the eruption of matter destroys health, undermines the body and reduces strength." (Ibid.)

Thus Clement of Alexandria considers against nature both heterosexual and homosexual coitus, in which ejaculation occurs but which is not directed toward conception. He even calls for sexual relations with his wife to be limited only to the production of children. And he considers non-creational methods of marital intercourse to be a sign of excessive fascination with sexuality. They can also be against nature because they sometimes involve an exchange of male (active) and female (passive) roles.

> "Luxury has deranged all things; it has disgraced man. A luxurious niceness seeks everything, attempts everything, forces everything, coerces nature. Men play the part of women, and women that of men, contrary to nature; women are at once wives and husbands: no passage is closed against libidinousness; and their promiscuous lechery is a public institution, and luxury is domesticated. O miserable spectacle!" (Idib. Book 3)

On this side, heterosexual vaginal intercourse with his wife turns out to be contrary to nature if the woman is on top (in the riding position). Interestingly, in some ancient collections of canon law, such sexual intercourse was punished as sodomy.

Of course, Clement condemns coitus between men. But not for the homosexual character, but for the uncreative waste of semen, the humiliation of the partner of a passive partner by a female role and excessive fascination with sexuality.

As arguments, he turns to archaic ideas about what is happening in the animal world and tries to comprehend biblical texts through his natural philosophical ideas. The modern reader cannot accept most of his arguments. For example, we now know that in the animal world, sexual intercourse serves not only for procreation. Homosexual behavior has also been recorded in the animal world.

The argument that a person does not have the right to additionally attribute social functions to natural organs and manifestations, to endow them with additional social meanings, also does not stand up to criticism. Even a contemporary of Clement's could have objected to him. "Really, don't we Christians greet each other with a holy kiss? Meanwhile, the natural structure of the mouth says that its natural purpose is to eat and make sounds, not to give kisses!"

With the help of the same archaic and not always thoughtful arguments, Clement recognizes as unnatural things that do not confuse most modern Christian fundamentalists. For example, shaving off a beard.

> "This, then, the mark of the man, the beard, by which he is seen to be a man, is older than Eve, and is the token of the superior nature. In this God deemed it right that he should excel, and dispersed hair over man's whole body. Whatever smoothness and softness was in him He abstracted from his side when He formed the woman Eve, physically receptive, his partner in parentage, his help in household management, while he (for he had parted with all smoothness) remained a man, and shows himself man... It is therefore impious to desecrate the symbol of manhood, hairiness... "But the very hairs of your head are all numbered", says the Lord (Matthew 10:30), those on the chin, too, are numbered, and those on the whole body. There must be therefore no plucking out, contrary to God's appointment, which has counted them in according to His will." (Ibid. Book 3)

Christians who insist that we must live according to archaic notions of the natural should consider what else the concept of "against nature" that Paul borrowed from his contemporary social concepts includes.

The first-century Jewish theologian Philo of Alexandria, discussing 18:22 and 20:13 of Leviticus, notes that they are constantly being violated by the Gentile people.

> "And I imagine that the cause of this is that among many nations there are actually rewards given for intemperance and effeminacy. At all events one may see men-women continually strutting through the market place at midday, and leading the processions in festivals; and, impious men as they are, having received by lot the charge of the temple, and beginning the sacred and initiating rites, and concerned even in the holy mysteries of Ceres." (Phylon of Alexandria. A Treatise on Those Special Laws Which Are Referrible to Two Commandments in the Decalogue, the Sixth and Seventh, Against Adulterers and All Lewd Persons, and Against Murderers and All Violence)

Now the important thing for us is that he criticizes the Gentiles for the same things as the apostle Paul. The unproductive waste of a man's seed is also a sin for him. He compares boy lovers to an ignorant farmer.

> "...like a worthless husbandman, he allows fertile and productive lands to lie fallow, contriving that they shall continue barren, and labours night and day at cultivating that soil from which he never expects any produce at all." (Ibid.)

We already said at the beginning of the book that in ancient times only the male seed was considered responsible for the formation of a child. The female body was perceived only as soil, providing material and nutrition for growth and development. Therefore, the useless waste of male semen in those days was taken much more seriously than now. It was almost tantamount to premeditated murder. Philo of Alexandria accuses boy lovers of almost genocide:

> "Let the man who is possessed by tAnd let the man who is devoted to the love of boys submit to the same punishment, since he pursues that pleasure which is contrary to nature, and

> since, as far as depends upon him, he would make the cities desolate, and void, and empty of all inhabitants, wasting his power of propagating his species..." (Ibid.)

He also fears that this barren "farming" feminizes boys and prevents them from developing masculinity. In his opinion, such boys "get used to being treated like women, and thus exhaust not only their souls but also their bodies, they do not arouse in themselves a single spark of masculine character that can be saved and then rekindled" (ibid.).

In the Greek text, the apostle Paul says that men do 'aschemosunen' on men. We can understand it as a metaphor for doing something obscene. But in reality this word means that men disfigure each other. And this is related to the fact that the participants in cult orgies (the apostle writes about idolatry, not abstract sexual relations) punish themselves in a certain way. Philo, a contemporary of Paul, illustrates precisely what this might mean.

> "And some of these persons have even carried their admiration of these delicate pleasures of youth so far that they have desired wholly to change their condition for that of women, and have castrated themselves and have clothed themselves in purple robes, like those who, having been the cause of great blessings to their native land, walk about attended by body-guards, pushing down every one whom they meet." (Ibid.)

Such effeminate men who castrated themselves and became priests of the goddess Cybele (Ceres, Astartes) were called galli. More details are provided by the 2nd century author Lucian in his treatise "On the Syrian Goddess":

> "On certain days a multitude flocks into the temple, and the Galli in great numbers, sacred as they are, perform the

> ceremonies of the men and gash their arms and turn their backs to be lashed. Many bystanders play on the pipes the while many beat drums; others sing divine and sacred songs. All this performance takes place outside the temple, and those engaged in the ceremony enter not into the temple. During these days they are made Galli. As the Galli sing and celebrate their orgies, frenzy falls on many of them and many who had come as mere spectators after wards are found to have committed the great act. I will narrate what they do. Any young man who has resolved on this action, strips off his clothes, and with a loud shout bursts into the midst of the crowd, and picks up a sword from a number of swords which I suppose have been kept ready for many years for this purpose. He takes it and castrates himself and then runs wild through the city, bearing in his hands what he has cut off. He casts it into any house at will, and from this house he receives women's raiment and ornaments. Thus they act during their ceremonies of castration."

This is exactly the picture of the folly of idolatry that Paul wanted to paint for his readers. The Roman addressees of the apostles understood this well. As early as 204 BC, the main sanctuary of Cybele was moved from Pessinunt in Upper Phrygia to Rome. Her symbol was also brought here: a black stone in the shape of a phallus. This is how the Romans tried to avoid defeat in the 2nd Punic War. The wife of the Roman emperor became the high priestess of Cybele. Five centers of worship of Cybele were founded in Rome itself. According to the poem "Fasti" (Calendar) by the ancient Roman poet Ovid (43 BC - 18 AD), sacred processions passed through the streets of Rome every April. Of course, they ended in ritual orgies. Paul's Roman addressees saw all this with their own eyes.

Now you realize that for them, it was a story not about the horror of homosexuality, but about the madness of idolatry? A story about a crazy obsession with sexual passion.

Paul shows the sexual insatiability of the Gentiles in many ways. Reasonable doses of marital sex are no longer enough for them. Therefore, they resort to unproductive methods of sexual intercourse — "against nature". In Paul's day, such methods were used as contraception and encouraged in brothels. But in the eyes of a righteous Jew or Christian, they were perceived as deliberate murder for pleasure. But this is not enough for idolaters. The sex-crazed pagan gods drove their worshipers to such madness that men maimed each other and castrated themselves for idols. In this sense, they themselves punished themselves for their idolatry.

Further evidence that for the ancient reader sex against nature in Paul's epistle meant not homosexuality but unproductive sexual intercourse is Aurelius Augustine's commentary on this passage:

> " As to what the apostle says of the wicked, that leaving the natural use of the woman, the men burned in their lust one toward another: men with men working that which is unseemly; Romans 1:27 he did not speak of the conjugal use, but the natural use, wishing us to understand how it comes to pass that by means of the members created for the purpose the two sexes can combine for generation. Thus it follows, that even when a man unites with a harlot to use these members, the use is a natural one. It is not, however, commendable, but rather culpable. But as regards any part of the body which is not meant for generative purposes, should a man use even his own wife in it, it is against nature and flagitious. Indeed, the same apostle had previously Romans 9:26 said concerning women: Even their women did change the natural use into that which is against nature; and then concerning men he

> added, that they worked that which is unseemly by leaving the natural use of the woman. Therefore, by the phrase in question, the natural use, it is not meant to praise conjugal connection; but thereby are denoted those flagitious deeds which are more unclean and criminal than even men's use of women, which, even if unlawful, is nevertheless natural." (Augustine of Hippo. On Marriage and Concupiscence, Book 2)

From this long explanation, it is clear that when he speaks of intercourse against nature, he does not mean kissing or any kind of sexual caresses, but he means penetration by the male organ without the intention of conception. For the Jews and Christians influenced by the Jewish tradition, non-productive forms of sex were associated with sexual excess. Because of the ancient understanding of the nature of conception, they were considered murder for the sake of contraception. If a man decides to kill for a dose of sexual pleasure, he is clearly abusing sex.

Even when Paul is indignant that men have left their wives and gone to other men, it does not mean to him or to his addressees that being gay is a sin. This is just another sign of sexual insatiability. Here is what the biblical scholar Stephen J. Patterson writes about it:

> "Most people today think that a man who has sex with a man must be gay. But ancients did not think this way. They did not know about sexual orientation — gay, straight, or bi. They assumed, rather, that a person's sexual appetite could be expressed with either gender. A person with a normal sex drive would usually have sex with a person of the opposite gender. But people with voracious sexual appetites and weak self-control might go further and have sex with a person of the same gender — excess sex, you might say. Same-gendered sex was not a sign that someone was homosexual. It meant that someone was lacking in self-control. That is how Paul thinks

of same-gendered sex". (Stephen J. Patterson. Paul Hated Sex (But Thought You Should Enjoy It)

So the passage in question is the apostle's monologue about the dire consequences of idolatry leading to sexual gluttony. Paul did not know about gays and did not write about them. From these verses it is impossible to derive ethical norms for gay Christians who love one another, far from idolatry, adultery and sexual obsession.

"Paul, it turns out, did not hate gay people. He did not yet know about gay people. What he hated was sex. To him, sex was just raw passion. One ought to be able to resist it. Sex is for spiritual sissies, he thought. But he knew that most of us are sissies, so he made a concession. In 1 Corinthians he writes, "it is better to marry than to be aflame with passion" (1 Corinthians 7:9). If Paul had known about the whole range of human sexuality, he would have despised all of that too, but perhaps no more than any other sexual expression. Perhaps he would have said to anyone, both straight and gay: "it is better to marry than to be aflame with passion." (Ibid.)

Can a Christian not be homophobic?

Remember what we agreed earlier (see chapter: "The key to Heaven's gate is love"): if it suddenly turns out that the Bible does not condemn same-sex sexual attraction, then same-sex love relationships are no worse than heterosexual love from a soteriological point of view. It's time to briefly summarize the analysis of biblical texts used by homonegativists.

Genesis 1:27. The phrase "male and female created he them" can be understood as a rhetorical device of merism. In this case, it is a declaration of bi-modality in human gender rather than binary. Such a reading is more in line with modern scientific knowledge and the inner features of the biblical text.

Genesis 2:23-24. Nothing in the Bible indicates that the marriage of Adam and Eve is the only type of marriage for all people for all time that God approves of. In contrast, certain features of Adam and Eve's marriage were later forbidden as sins (e.g., incest). Additionally, the Bible contains examples of marriages that do not conform to the Adam and Eve model (the polygamy of the Old Testament saints). Finally, the Bible proclaims the principle of freedom: people can do anything except that which is harmful and sinful (1 Corinthians 6:12; 10:23). In relation to marriage, this means that people are free to decide for themselves what kind of marital relationship they can or cannot have. The most important thing is that their understanding of marriage does not harm their spiritual life and does not lead to sin.

Genesis, chapter 19. The biblical account of the destruction of Sodom does not mention homosexuality.The attempt of the inhabitants (both men and women) to rape Lot's guests is sinful by the very fact of the violence, regardless of homo- or hetero-orientation. In the places in the

Bible where the sins of Sodom are listed, there is no mention of same-sex relationships.

Jude's statement that the Sodomites sought another body does not fit the description of the essence of homosexuality, which is the pursuit of the same body and not another. He probably means that because of their xenophobia, they unknowingly attacked the angelic body. However, this expression can also be understood as an allusion to zoophilia or cheating on one's wife. In the latter case, "another body" must mean "a different body than that intended for that person."

Leviticus 18:22; 20:13. If we believe the letter of the traditional European translations, there is no prohibition against lying with a man — it is forbidden to lie with a man as with a woman (in a feminine way). In the ancient view, this means that a man should not take on a passive (female) role, and should not encourage another man to do so.

In their Jewish tradition, these prohibitions have two versions of translation and understanding: either as a prohibition on sexual intercourse with men who also have female organs (with hermaphrodites), or as a prohibition on several men lying together with one woman. Furthermore, the prohibitions are expressed to avoid the idolatrous traditions practiced by Israel's neighbors. It is unforgivably reckless to automatically extend them to the ethics of love relationships between Christians who are far from idolatry.

1 Corinthians 6:9; 1 Timothy 1:10. There is no compelling argument why Paul's neologism "arsenokoites" and the metaphor of "malakia" should be associated with homosexual habits. Early translations contained many alternative meanings unrelated to homosexuality. Patriarch of Constantinople f the Faster writes that the sin of arsenoscoity can be committed by men and their wives. The fact is that today no one knows exactly what the apostle Paul meant. A hypothesis that is no more convincing than many other alternatives is not suitable for a conclusion that greatly affects the lives of millions of people. We must be very careful with the letters of the apostle Paul, "wherein are some things hard to be understood, which the ignorant and unstedfast wrest, as they do also the other scriptures, unto their own destruction (2 Peter 3:16)."

Romans 1:26-27. The apostle Paul is not writing about homosexuality, but about sexual obsession, which he says is caused by idolatry. The expression "using (something) against nature" in the understanding of the time did not refer to homosexual acts, but to the unproductive shedding of semen. Even men switching from women to men is not a sign of homosexuality (of which they knew nothing) but a sign of sexual licentiousness, according to Paul and his contemporaries. The Apostle Paul disliked sex in general. After all, to have legitimate sex you had to take on the responsibilities of marriage and family, which distract from serving the Lord (1 Corinthians 7:32-34). Ideally, Paul thought, it would be better to remain single, as he was (1 Corinthians 7:1,7-8). But the apostle was a realist and understood that not everyone is called to the feat of abstinence. If Paul had modern scientific knowledge about the nature of human sexuality and understood that homosexual acts could be not only a sign of sexual overeating, but also a symptom of an innate orientation, the same as a heterosexual, it is very likely that he would say the same to homosexuals as to heterosexuals who do not have to the virginity of a vocation:

> "But if they have not continency, let them marry: for it is better to marry than to burn!" (1 Corinthians 7:9)

The only Christian value is the ability to love selflessly and devotedly. Only it has a soteriological meaning and remains unchanged at all times and in eternity.

> "Love never faileth: but whether there be prophecies, they shall be done away; whether there be tongues, they shall cease; whether there be knowledge, it shall be done away". (1 Corinthians 13:8)

Unfortunately, Christian fundamentalists have declared as Christian values the forms of adaptation of people to the conditions of a corrupt world, which change historically and have no soteriological significance. Therefore, they fight for the immutability and preservation of these external forms, while the calling of Christians is completely opposite: to gradually change the external conditions and forms of human life and the structure of society so that they more and more correspond to the ideal of the only and true Christian value — love!

Having confused content with form, immutable values with external methods of its implementation, which change depending on the circumstances, homonegativists, unnoticed by themselves, approached anti-Christian pastoral practices. When talking about heterosexuals, they agree that not everyone is called to the feat of abstinence. They can agree with us that marriage is a social form useful for spiritual life, in which people who do not have a vocation to virginity can respectfully realize their sexual needs and develop the capacity for Christian love. With a little thought, they will even agree that having children is not a requirement of every godly marriage. That the command to be fruitful and multiply in the person of Adam and Eve was given to all mankind, not to each individual. And that many people (among them the apostles of Christ) did not fulfill this command for various reasons, but pleased God and have hope of salvation.

However, as soon as the conversation turns to homosexuals, these same people forget that not everyone is called to abstinence and that the justification for marriage can be not only the birth of a child, but also the desire to calm one's sexuality in godly marital intimacy, as the Apostle Paul taught ("that Satan tempt you not because of your incontinency" 1 Corinthians 7:5). Then, instead of giving homosexual couples space to develop in Christian love, instead of addressing them with the New Testament principle "it is better to marry than to be inflamed with passion" (see: 1 Corinthians 7:9), homonegativists excommunicate homosexuals from marriage, pushing them into a sinful life.

Heterosexual homonegativists place unbearable burdens on homosexual Christians (see: Luke 11:46) that they themselves are not prepared to bear.

By forcing homosexuals to live in a way they do not have the strength to live, fundamentalists push them to sin. After this, for this sin they promise homosexuals eternal torment in hell, but at the same time they themselves do not hear Christ's warning to them:

> "But whoso shall cause one of these little ones that believe on me to stumble, it is profitable for him that a great millstone should be hanged about his neck, and that he should be sunk in the depth of the sea." (Matthew 18:6)

But Christians who want to fight for the true Christian value of love must support the desire of same-sex couples to live in committed, monogamous marriages.

9 798227 182678

9 798227 182678

Printed by Libri Plureos GmbH in Hamburg, Germany